Diary of Golden Leaves
My Love of Autumn
Becky Hall
©2016

Diary of Golden Leaves
 Copyright 2016
All rights reserved.

ISBN-13:
978-1533393760

ISBN-10:
1533393761

The information provided in this book is designed to provide helpful information on the subjects discussed. This book is not meant to be used, nor should it be used, to diagnose or treat any medical condition. For diagnosis or treatment of any medical problem, consult your own physician. The publisher and author are not responsible for any specific health or allergy needs that may require medical supervision and are not liable for any damages or negative consequences from any treatment, action, application or preparation, to any person reading or following the information in this book.